UTTER BALLS

Geoffrey Leet

To To:
hey best Thursday
Girl friend

Geoffrey

GW00702401

ARTHUR H. STOCKWELL LTD.
Torrs Park   Ilfracombe   Devon
Established 1898
www.ahstockwell.co.uk

By the same author:
From Bulls to Balls
From Furrows to Fairways
Amanda

ISBN 0 7223 3635-7
Printed in Great Britain by
Arthur H. Stockwell Ltd.
Torrs Park   Ilfracombe
Devon

UTTER BALLS

The Changing Face of Golf Clubs

Eighty years ago a Golf Club used to consist of some hundred fanatic golfers, most of whom were city men, well-trousered, who could afford the £10 to £20 which was the annual sub of that era.

The course was looked after by at least six or seven men who graduated from the farms and knew what a bit of good coloured grass was all about. They mowed the greens with machines that they pushed by hand and to get around the whole eighteen holes often took over two days with four men doing the shoving.

The Club House was rough (and not always ready) and log fires and plenty of whisky kept the few Members reasonably happy. The Members were looked after by a man and his wife who generally lived in the village and more often than not had another main job on the side. The wife, when she had the time from her own house, would come along and cook some home-made cakes, and on a weekend there was generally a leg of lamb and a couple of veg for those who were on the course for the day and didn't want to go back home. Drink was more often than not left out for the Member to help himself and he always wrote down what he had taken in the Drinks Book provided.

There was the Secretary who was definitely part-time and generally turned up on the weekend and only then when the

3

bar was manned. To be fair to him, there wasn't a lot for him to do. There were no such things as the Monthly Medal; that was to come. There was the odd match either between Members or even more rare, between other Clubs and here of course the Secretary came into his own and checked what cards had been handed in and, over further noggins, announced the winners for the day. He had some office work to do when the annual subs were due and very rarely he attended a Committee meeting and took some notes which were never circulated and quite often were lost by the time that the next yearly meeting occurred. But it didn't really matter, everyone was frightfully matey and what someone said a year ago, or thought he did, could always be said again.

As to how the course became a course was a matter between a few enthusiasts who took clubs out onto a field, with the permission of the farmer, and gradually worked out the plan of the place from tee to green. They then bought the land, and over the years someone would suggest that a bunker should go here, because old General Smith always bounced his drive around about that spot and anyway his handicap was suspect and had been for years.

They were not interested in making a profit; they were not particularly worried if they made a loss for the year. The Hon Treasurer would get up at the AGM, which was well-attended if a dozen turned up, and say that really they ought to find a few hundred here and there and could he have it by the next month or two. Members then wrote cheques out and the red figure turned overnight to black. It was so nice and easy and oh so leisurely.

Now in 1976 the wheel has turned very much full circle, and it is doubtful if any comparison could be made with the past form of golf. As a Secretary and owner of a Golf Club and one who travels round other Clubs, the whole set up is becoming more and more of a rat race, and you cannot help wondering how things are going to turn out.

When I started this place life was fairly easy, I was constructing, with the help of one kind chap, some eighteen holes, and Members were pouring in even before the barley had been taken off the last few acres. But then you see I only had a hundred or so trusting Members and when I wasn't laying out a green, I was pouring out a drink in the bar. When my wife wasn't taking the kids to school, she was in the cook house playing about with a steak for some hungry Member. One could cope and it was all great fun planning ahead to do the things that would one day make the place into something that people would be glad to belong to.

I was lucky too, for my tractor driver, who was a lousy ploughman (he and I used to compete in the local ploughing match and I always seemed to come in ahead of him), he saw that the plough wouldn't be used anymore, so turned his hand to making bunkers instead. My cowman thought nothing of this lark, for though sheep, of which we had some 300, would just fit in with golf, cows were certainly a drawback, and after one of his prize heifers was struck smartly up the rear end by a ball travelling at over 100 miles an hour, he took off to saner climes.

I also lost my shepherd for the same reason, not a driven ball, but it was the question of, for the want of a better word, manure. Having sold the cows, the sheep and the golfers were on terms of armed neutrality. From my point of view they, the sheep, were doing the course a lot of good. A sheep is the best machine made to convert tough old cocksfoot into something manageable, but they do have this habit of lying down at night and getting rid of the day's fodder whilst in a recumbent position. That was serious enough, but they also had the idea that the warm sand of a bunker was just the place to 'pull the chain', so to speak. Then next day some wandering golfer through, let's face it his own fault, would miss the green and land in a bunker which was full of this brown stuff and it soon became apparent that either the golfer would give up and go elsewhere, which seemed silly after what had been done, or the cattle-carrier would come along one morning and my 300 ewes and their lambs would depart for the local market.

So that is how the shepherd went, with, of course, all my

sheep, lambs, rams, the lot. The place seemed a lot quieter after that though I must admit I missed them more than I thought I would. I cannot say that I had the same feelings when the cows went; we were at that stage of constructing a Golf Course, milking some 1,000 pints per day from forty to fifty animals, bottling it all and delivering it to various housewives. It was a great relief when the last bottle was filled and for that matter delivered.

I am not, to be honest, sure whether I was glad to see the back of the cows or the housewives, the former were time-consuming and the latter in some cases impossible. Those of you who have not had the undoubted pleasure of getting up at 'sparrow's fart', as it is called in the country for some reason best known to the birds, and wandering round the quiet countryside disturbing the peace with a thousand clanking bottles, should have a go, it divorces the mind from other troubles that it might have collected.

The idiosyncrasies of the British housewife as regards to her thoughts about milk are legion. She has the thought that milk, unless it is boiled, fried or generally fiddled about with, is deadly poison and that she will lose every baby she is starting to carry. She also has the idea that her nails will drop out and that her hair will become peculiar. It isn't enough for her to ask her milkman to leave her pint at the front door, she also has other ideas as to where it should be left, for instance the back door, by the garage, on a shelf, in a dovecote or in a dog kennel (always with a bloody great dog in it). There were some who always said that she would leave the kitchen door open and would I just pop in and leave it in the fridge — 'there's a dear'. I learnt the hard way with the latter idea, for the good lady had forgotten to tell her husband this labour-saving thought and he caught me creeping out one early dawn — it was an interesting five minutes!

Looking back on all this one wonders as to how one even sold a pint to anyone, but a certain low cunning came to my aid and on wet days, when I could do no other work, I used to get out the car and follow the local milkman on his rounds. I made a note of where he dropped four pints (I forgot the one pint lady, she really wasn't worth it and probably paid her bills once a year). I would then go back later in the day, when the husband had gone to work, dressed as the best-clothed cowman in Kent with a pint of last night's milk with a cream line three times the length of the stuff that was still probably sitting on her doorstep. After a cautious opening of the door by the lady of the house, her immediate reaction was to shut it even quicker for I looked a sight with muddy gumboots and the faint wisp of straw stuck in my cap, *but* the incongruous thing about the whole scene which always seemed to intrigue the good lady was my accent. I have the idea that it is known as 'plumy' or certainly very much 'BBC 2', but it should certainly never emerge from such a peculiar-looking figure and this always seemed to prevent her slamming the door. I then used to point at her four pints and ask her as to whether she knew how old they were and for that matter when they had last seen their owner, the cow. To this question she had no answer. I then pointed to my pint held in my grubby hand and invited her and her family to come and see how it was all done that afternoon up at the farm. In this way we reached our thousand pints but I must say that we didn't just stick to milk, there were hens from which we had a few eggs, but demand soon outstripped the supply and we had to go to a friend who kept thousands of birds in cages.

When families went on holiday there was the question of what to do with their dogs. This seemed to fit in just right as we had large barns doing nothing and so the dog racket started in conjunction with the milk, and although I feel that the powers that be would not have approved, it was quite normal from our point of view to depart with our thousand full bottles at crack of dawn and come back with a thousand empty ones plus a couple of fighting dogs.

The wife or owner of our dog is a bit peculiar about her pet. She has the idea that just no other food would do for her animal but the stuff she bought in a tin. Having enquired from me before the holiday was due as to whether I used her particular type of tin, to which I, through force of habit, always used to say that I didn't, she would leave out at least half-a-dozen cans for the poor starving animal for me to give her/him whilst he was incarcerated in my barns. What she didn't seem to understand was that to shift an animal from one spot to another and give it someone else to smell, puts it off its feed for a couple of days anyway, so that if you have the thing for a week, the feed bill is quite low.

We got up to about twenty dogs at any one time and found the thought of exercising each, one at a time, was not on, we just didn't have the number of hours available during the day, so we wired in about ten acres and used to turn the lot out in one fell swoop, hoping that the large ones wouldn't eat the small and that we would round them up by dusk.

I must say that the somewhat timid Peke-like animal, whose only exercise before she came to us was a short, not very sharp, stroll down to the supermarket, wore quite a surprised expression after a couple of days of open air. What happened when she went back to a somewhat different life at the end of the family holiday I don't know.

Also along with our milk went learned discussions with the master of the house concerned, who thought that all farmers were natural gardeners and did I know why his garden wouldn't grow anything. The obvious answer to this one was muck and more muck and thus another small avenue of income was given to us. The muck delivering was usually done on the Sunday when we didn't deliver milk, not I hasten to add because of any religious fervour but because we delivered a double lot on the Saturday which took some doing, and so I got a day off to catch up with other work which was always having the habit of being left behind.

The muck handling from our end was quite simple in that one of the tractors had a grab on the front and with a bit of luck you could get two tons into a farm trailer in four or five bites. I then trundled the whole, somewhat smelly, lot to the milk customer who had a lousy garden, and with the aid of hydraulics I used to tip the lot into his front patch.

I got into trouble once where, incautiously backing my load, I thought that everything was clear and tipped the lot over the family pram. The child I am glad to say had been taken out to have the usual clean up of the back end, but there was no doubt about the pram, it was in a mess and what you could see of it smelt like no pram should. They were good customers, had four pints every day, had two nice large dogs and went away as often as they could, so the obvious thing to do was to go out and buy another pram, which we did.

One would have thought that was the end of what a farmer could do for his milk customers, but there was the question of garden stakes and bean poles and fire wood. All of which was delivered at odd times whenever we could spare a minute, and all of which again helped to bring in more cash to get on with the building of the Golf Course.

With the fire wood we got to the stage of cutting the stuff at home and inviting the prospective wood-burner to bring his car down and fill his boot. This was a lot easier than delivering the stuff and as long as one cut the customer down to size, so that if he wanted to fill a small van, that was one price and an ordinary car boot was another.

At this time, having got a few large contracts for milk, I found myself trying to get rid of them as there just wasn't the time or for that matter the milk. Also some places that shall be nameless would take in a couple of churns of milk, ask for two empty ones and water down our nice creamy milk in double the quantity that we were paid for. I had the feeling that when they were found out the blame would be smartly turned in my direction.

I eased my way out of all of them with the exception of the catering people who ran Brands Hatch. They had been our first large customers, and used to take up to 100 gallons of milk per day and really had started us on the right path. I felt that I must last out as long as I could till they found another chump who would do what I did every race meeting. They would ring up a few days before the meeting and say that they wanted the usual 100 gallons delivered, generally on a

Saturday. This entailed a lot of planning as we had all our normal (or nearly normal) households to deliver to by about 11.00 and the Hatch wanted their milk at about 6 a.m. I had a large one-ton van at that time which would take ten churns with ease and I used to arrive at the race track at about 4 a.m. This used to cause some concern to the various security-minded gentlemen who were paid to keep everyone out of the place during the hours of darkness; they also had large dogs who if not paid, certainly helped. I had about seven small cafes, for want of a better word, where the milk had to be delivered and they were all right on the edge of the track. After satisfying the various truncheon-carrying guards and their howling dogs I would set off to deliver my clanking churns. I soon found out that the easiest way to deliver the stuff was to get onto the track itself, and by some little effort get a ten-gallon churn over, through and sometimes under the safety barrier and thus into the cafe. The guards didn't think much of this idea but after I had started unloading the fourth churn in their office for them to deliver they changed their minds and I was allowed onto the track.

The last time that I had been on a racetrack was on the mountain track at Brooklands, where really I suppose I learnt something about handling a car, but that is another story, and nothing about delivering milk. So there I was clanking around Brands Hatch in a one-ton van, watched by anxious guards in case I did the wrong thing, and from my point of view in a hell of a hurry for I had several hundred housewives to satisfy, all of whom wanted their milk on time delivered at the front door/back door/dovecote/dog kennel etc., etc.

One glorious morning when the dawn was about to crack and I had nearly finished delivering my last churn, I was overtaken by a racing car out for an early track exercise. I was a bit late and he was a bit early but I shall never forget the look on his helmeted face as he had to pull out to overtake a van doing a lumbering 20 mph.

All this time the Golf Course was gradually taking shape and thousands of turves would be delivered in each week for us to lay on the greens that we had prepared. I preferred turf to seed for one or two reasons, one being that with a bit of luck they would knit together and the course would be playing long before a seeded area would bear the weight of a studded fourteen stone golfer, also I wanted to know what I was buying and what was easier than to see a field at least seven years old of the very stuff that I had been looking for. I looked at various bowling greens and saw what they were made of, and I also looked at Wimbledon and saw what that was made of and found out where they got their turf from when they wanted to patch a court at the end of the season. This is what I wanted, something fine, but hard-wearing and this is what I got.

I was also faced with the question of the fairways and what to do with them, for by this time we had several greens finished and also various tees but nothing in between. I had ploughed the lot after harvest and the land had been left in the ploughed state with the exception of one small area that I had had the time to disc, harrow and roll, but with the lack of hard cash which was all going into the greens, I hadn't been able to sow it down to what I hoped would be the ley of all times.

Having a quick look at this area one day I was struck by the number of natural grasses that were appearing, the bents and the fescues and a host more, also a fair number of weeds were competing for light. But the main thing was that if one had the courage to view this in the future, there seemed to be no difference in this natural sward to some of the fairways that I tramped around. So when the weather was right, I took a chance, levelled the lot, shut the gates and firmly forgot all about it.

Looking back on this episode of the making of a Golf Course, it wasn't as mad as it seemed, for years ago before the war I had sat in the saddle of what used to be called a Waler in Australia, driving cows and their calves from one end of a little place 900 miles west of Brisbane called Windorah. The cattle station itself was mostly desert and the owners paid the Government the large sum of one halfpenny per year per square mile, they also had to keep the fences up.

On those 4,000 square miles I learnt a bit about this and that and I shall never forget the natural grasses that used to spring up after one of the rare rainfalls that occurred in that somewhat bleak area. So if grass could grow in that sort of heat, why should it not grow in our sort of climate!

So that was how most of the fairways were made. I must admit that on one or two I sowed some excellent very expensive seed at about the rate of about 75 lbs per acre, but to my mind the self-sown material is more springy, looks better and what more seems to hold a ball up in a manner which helps the golfer.

It took about six months to plan out the first nine, lay out the greens, turf them and do the same with the tees. By this time the so-called fairway was starting to show some seed heads which we promptly swiped off so that further seeds could grow and thicken the place up a bit. We applied fertiliser at the rate of about 2 cwt per acre to all the fairways and followed this up with either nitro chalk or ammonia, in fact more or less exactly the same as we did with the cows and the sheep and for that matter the corn as well.

About July, just six months after we had started, we invited the Members to have a go and with great ceremony four brave types drove off the first nine holes. The greens were as rough as old boots, tramlines were everywhere but nobody seemed to mind and seemed glad that we had got along so fast.

I had by this time well over 100 Members, of which some fifty had attended the first public meeting that I thought I had better hold to see whether there was in fact any demand for a Golf Course at all. This was held in the Otford Village Hall and the hire of the hall in those days was £1 for the evening. I remember paying the fee and wondering as to whether anyone would turn up. I had inserted various notices in the local papers, and for good measure and to lend a bit of tone to the place I imported my solicitor and my accountant, the former to answer any legal questions and the latter to deal with the cash side, if of course there was going to be any cash.

I knew that at least six would turn up because it was they

who used to come along on a Sunday when we were still farming and ask whether they could knock a golf ball about over the fields. I always let them but used to make quite sure that they knew in what field I had a certain bull called Churchill. This chap was an Angus, which meant that he had no horns but also as bulls go he was fairly small but had a turn of speed that would have made a greyhound look to its laurels. He also, like most of his breed, was intensely curious about anything that seemed to him to be odd.

On one particular Sunday when our six stalwarts had gone out with the usual warnings about Churchill, one came tearing back after half an hour or so and said that they were having trouble with my bull and would I do something about him *now*. So I dropped everything and went and took a look, and there was Churchill stamping on a set of clubs and roaring his head off. The owner of the clubs with some dexterity had leaped a fence but had wisely decided to make certain of getting over and had dropped his clubs so as to be sure of clearing the three strands of barbed wire. With some low cunning and the entry into the field of a bulling heifer, we persuaded Churchill to stop destroying the clubs and get on with the work of providing crossbred beef calves. I mention these six chaps because I suppose it was they, right after the bull episode, who persuaded me to get on with the idea of making a Golf Course and to 'get rid of those bloody bulls'.

Anyway I digress more than usual, let's get back to the meeting where I expected some six gentlemen and maybe a stray dog to turn up. I arranged lots of chairs without much hope of filling them and took my two paid professionals next door where there was a pub to give them some Dutch courage. We dallied maybe a bit and were interrupted by one of the six faithful who came in and asked when I was going to start. I thought he was being funny, but he stated that the place was filling up fast and there must have been two hundred people in the hall now and more were coming, and did I have any more chairs!

So we downed the last pint and rushed back, and how right

he was, the place was packed with serious-looking gents and even the odd female could be seen. We galloped up to the stage in a cloud of beer fumes and sat ourselves down and tried to look respectable. For after all who knows all these chaps might have cheque books at the ready and could be future Members!

I was very conscious of the interested faces underneath our small stage and it wasn't hard to guess that they were wondering as to what this chap had to sell in the way of Golf Courses. Was he honest? Did he know what he was talking about? I stood all this for a few minutes and then taking a deep breath, stood up. I am probably lucky in that a crowd of people doesn't make me nervous. The only time that I get that way is when I feel that I have to prepare a long speech, then I do start to feel uncertain. But now, bar for a few rough notes I had prepared nothing. It was all in my mind what I wanted to do and it came tumbling out in no great order, but I presume with some impact on the people who were listening as there wasn't a murmur till I had finished.

I then asked my solicitor to say a word and he did just that and sat down again. So I invited questions from the floor and they came thick and fast. Things that I never thought about; for instance, what Committees would I be having? Who was going to be the Pro? What was I personally going to do? How much money had I got? They didn't get much change out of that one as I was more that usually broke at the time, but I felt that was my business, so I hedged on that one.

This all went on for about an hour till I thought that they had had enough, so I took the plunge and asked for a show of hands on the motion that if I built a Golf Course, would they back me. To my astonishment all hands seemed to leap in the air and then everyone started to clap which was embarrassing. So we went in a great throng to the nearest pub and celebrated just about six months too soon, for it was in that time we opened the first nine holes.

After this some money started pouring in. Enough certainly to buy the necessary turf and start laying the place out to what we had planned really on the back of a Player packet in a pub some six months before.

I can always remember our first member, the very first chap who waved a cheque book at me and said how much did I want. I hadn't even started the place properly, I think we had laid a green or two but the barley was all over the place uncut. There I was perched on top of a roaring dusty combine when along comes this fellow wanting to join. Farmers become somewhat different people when the harvest starts, they are not really pleasant people to live with. They have taken endless trouble to produce a field of corn, have defied the Good Lord who has sent rain and storms to knock it down, have found that the combine, after leaving it completely alone for the best part of a year with not the slightest bit of attention, reluctant to start, and although the corn is ripe to cut and the moisture content is looking fine, there are storm clouds about and you just don't want to stop for anyone. But this chap just stood right in the middle of the patch that I was about to cut and held up his hand like a copper on the road. So fuming slightly I yelled to him to either get the hell out of it or let me know in two seconds flat what he wanted. And there it was our first offer of cash which had nothing to do with horns or hooves, milk bottles, muck or what you will. We were in the golfing business.

We struck lucky after a month or two of building the course because our next-door neighbours, who lived in a long sort of building covered with ivy, came along and asked us whether we would like to buy the place. They were asking £4,000 and after taking a look around the place which was in a very peculiar state, I said yes we would. They were Irish, or at least she was. They had lived there for thirty years and had never had a dustbin or for that matter a bath in that time. We discovered in fact that it had been an old Club House and had been shut down in 1942.

I am one of these odd people who actually likes the Irish but their habits never cease to amaze me, for it soon became apparent that they had to do something with their rubbish and they found that the easiest way was to open one of the many locker doors in the place and fling their tins in, shutting the door smartly before the pile started to emerge again. They must have had shares in tin because after they had gone in a cloud of dust one day, we took some twenty-trailer loads of rubbish out of the place. How they or I should say she, survived being electrocuted I have no idea because if you held an ordinary 40 watt bulb to their cooking stove it gave quite a healthy glow, but maybe it was the gumboots that stood beside the cooker which she said she always wore that saved her hide.

So what with making a course, we set to in what little spare time we had left to create a Club House. After we took the rubbish out we got hold of a firm of plumbers and inserted new pipes and radiators all over the place, built the bar up ourselves, went to the local market and purchased a lot of armchairs that all needed new covers, but as we didn't pay more that £5 for any chair, the bill wasn't too bad. We purchased carpets in the same way and for around about £6,000 we had a Club House that had a certain amount of rustic charm, and finally got hold of a brewer who installed us with pump and beer and somewhat grudgingly, a few glasses.

By this time we were up to about 200 Members. I was fortunate that at the start of all of this I was quite determined that because the place belonged to my wife and myself no Committee were going to make rules of their own without being vetted first. This was because it fairly soon became apparent that various cliques made noises on and off the stage that the place was really a Members' Club and we were a bit in the way. So I drew up a set of rules which I made everyone sign, even the first lot who had come in, making it quite clear that I didn't mind a hoot how many Committees they, the Members, wanted to have, but the results of the lot *must* come through the office first. We had one resignation out of the 200 which wasn't bad.

I found myself manning the bar, the greens and for good measure the office as well. My wife would do the breakfasts on the weekend and quite often dinner at night. I found myself getting down bottles of Scotch at a much faster rate than I wished. The trouble was that everyone seemed so friendly and insisted that I drink with them and refused to let me pay for a round as they said that I couldn't afford it. I tried saying that really I had to work and would they mind drinking on their own, but this didn't work, they thought that one wasn't mixing in enough. So I finally went over to the old dodge of making up a bottle that looked like whisky but was merely water and a dash or two of pink. It tasted foul but I did at least end up sober at the end of the day much to the surprise of some of the more hardened drinkers.

Sometime about now I had also to make a decision as to whether I should call everyone by their Christian name, and of course vice versa, or stick to the more formal Mr, etc. I found that I had to tell a lot of people what to do, and even more important, what not to do and decided rightly or wrongly that I would be formal and *never* in the Club House or as you might call it 'on duty', call anyone by their first name. Ten years ago I had a few hurt looks because I wouldn't become one of the boys but now I have no regrets, it has paid off, lonely maybe, but I would do the same thing again if I had the choice.

I was then faced with the fact that although the course was coming on a pace, the tramlines on the greens had gone, and the fairways were starting to take shape, albeit a somewhat straight one which I would alter later on, but I had no way of watering the greens except by miles of hose ending up with a sprinkler on just one green. You might place this sprinkler on one particular patch of the green at 10.00, but you could bet by 11.00 some idiot golfer had shifted it because it got in the way of his putt, and you would go up later to shift it, only to find it placidly watering a bunker. Also my hose and the studs of the golfers never got on — you soon found little jets of water coming up all over the place where some dear chap had trodden on the hose. So I phoned all the automatic watering people and asked them to come along and give me a quote.

B

Our system to be was a bit 'Heath Robinson' because I inherited a fairly deep bore right outside my back door, some 240 feet deep and with about thirty feet of water in it at most times of the year. Having in my farming days obtained a licence to abstract water from it, it seemed daft at the time that although you owned the land and the water that fell on it went down below anyway, God help you if you abstracted as much as a pint without getting permission first. But anyway it seemed silly not to incorporate it into whatever system we might finally come round to.

Our old manor house, with miles of gutters and acres of cellars had to dispose of its surplus water somewhere, so through various downpipes it all drained off into a large underground holding tank complete with wrought iron hand pump, and all that, at the back door. This seemed at the time to be an ideal place into which I could store my water for the course. Beside this tank we installed a couple of pumps and placed the guts of the machine in our old garage at the back of the house. The guts is probably the wrong word for what is really a fine piece of modern technical know-how. You can program however many minutes you want each green to have, what time you want to water, etc., etc.

I used to make ghastly errors with the timing and one would be greeted with a moderately-annoyed soaked Member, who when addressing his putt on some green or other would have a solid jet of water flung up his backside, and as we were working at some 180 pounds per square inch, it did have the habit of spoiling his line.

We made the well work itself by placing a couple of wires, one negative and one positive, down to the water level, so that when the water 240 foot below rose by the action of the underground springs, it touched the positive wire which was connected to a submersible pump and up the water came. Likewise when the water sunk to a level about three foot above the bottom of the pump, the negative wire would be uncovered and the pump would switch itself off.

To see what sort of spread the sprinklers had on the green I used to, much to the horror of Albert the then head green keeper, throw down a gallon or so of a coloured vegetable dye, generally red, and you soon saw if one head wasn't doing what it was there for. I must admit that at times my long-suffering Members used to come along all looking very worried and insist that we had some terrible disease on the greens and what was I going to do about it!

I also hit on the idea of checking how much water went on each green by merely putting a rain gauge on a green last thing at night and then going along the next morning before the golfers arrived to see what was in it. Green keepers always have the idea that if you can flood a green all the better, but I cannot say that I agree with this and would rather see, depending on the state of the weather, roundabout three to four mm on each green each night.

The watering system cost with all its bits in the region of £12,000, so to date I had spent £6,000 on making a Golf Course, the same on the Club House, making a total of £24,000 and by this time I was trying to please some 500 Members.

On the subject of trying to please, I think that one can do just a bit too much. You cannot, however long-suffering you are, however efficient, please more than about 70% of your Members. I can remember getting frightfully worried when some serious chap would come along and ask as to whether he could see me in the office as he had a complaint. It was generally the loo paper was too hard, although you would the next day get some vast chap who would expound at length that the same handy material was far too soft.

Of course the beer and spirits were always far too costly in the Club House and I must be making a fortune. So at times when driven just a wee bit too far I would invite half-a-dozen of the complainers to come out on a round of the local pubs, and I would buy them what they wanted *if* they could find a pub where the prices were cheaper than ours, otherwise they would buy me what I wanted. I only did it twice, after that there were no more takers, but on the other hand I was in no fit state the next morning.

So there we were with quite a nice new Golf Course, the greens were coming on well and even the fairways, which if you remember were never sown with any purchased grass seed, were showing signs of promise. In places you were able to spread your hand on the newly-grown natural grasses and on taking the hand away, the imprint would remain for a while.

One of our main problems were flints. When I had farmed the place I used to wear out plough shares by the dozen and man-sized flints would appear to grow up all over the place. They were nice for drainage, for we didn't have a single ditch on nearly three hundred acres, but not so pleasant when Members complained that their best irons were being ruined by these wretched stones. So I went out and bought myself the biggest roller that I could find; one which my tractors could pull. You must consider that whilst farming we wanted a tractor to pull as much as possible, and this was made easier if the treads on the tyres were really thick and would bite into the ground. But having ruddy great treads on a Golf Course would mean the complaints would again come rolling in that the lie of their ball had been ruined by my tractor tyres. So all the tyres were changed to smooth-faced ones with no tread at all and then you had to have a rethink as to when you *could* get onto the ground without slipping and tearing the grass up by the roots.

Gradually we got the hang of it, the roller did its stuff and the flints were pushed into the ground. Of course during the spring and summer the fairways were cut every week and the resulting cut grass would fly behind the mowers and settle down to make a nice thick sward. On the other hand, we learned the hard way that it was quite silly to just roll and cut grass as the soil became impacted with the flints now well under some six inches of turf. The drainage suffered, so once again I had to buy another large machine that spiked the fairways down to some six inches or more so as to let the air in and let the water drain away.

By this time life was becoming somewhat hectic for Albert and I as there never seemed to be enough hours of daylight available to complete all the work. The greens, if one rushed around a bit and didn't stop for Members, would take two and a half to three hours every other day, and when the growing season was in full spate they were cut every day. It was easy, or easier, for me to mow the greens, as I could pull a large amount of rank if a Member got stroppy. If they wanted me to hang around whilst they lined up an approach shot, or a putt, it would have put at least an hour or more on the time taken to mow all the eighteen greens while not forgetting to give the winter greens a passing cut as one went by. It wasn't so easy for Albert when he was mowing as Members would tend to shout a bit, claiming their game was being spoiled, and so generally it used to take him quite a bit longer to do the same job.

It didn't happen often, but just now and then some dear Member would take a shot at the green knowing full well that you could be hit by a ball travelling at over a hundred miles per hour. When this did happen, I used to get off the mower, leaving it firmly in the way of any other shots, and tread somewhat heavily towards the man concerned wearing a somewhat puce-looking face. When I was some two inches away I would invite him to leave his clubs where they were and come and sit on the mower and I would try and see if I could make the green using his iron. I would even offer to teach him how to mow the green if he so wished, all with no charge whatsoever.

Among other jobs that were a must was the caning of the greens every morning. This consisted of wielding a long pliable cane and swishing off the dew, for dew and greens don't go together, you tend to get nasty diseases before you know where you are. You shifted the tee boxes at the same time. Both the Ladies' and the Men's tees needed a fresh patch of grass every day as otherwise the wear would be considerable. I used to fill up the tee boxes with loam and paint little notices on the side of the tee box inviting Members to fill in their own divots with the soil provided. Some did, some didn't, the latter thought that as they had paid their subs, then all they had to do was to play golf.

One of the many mistakes I made when we constructed the course was the size of the tees; they were like matchboxes and were worn out within the first few weeks of spring play. So I got down and constructed tees the same length as a cricket pitch, both for the men and the women, and as far as I can remember they were about eighteen inches wide and had nice gradual slopes all round so that the gang-mowers could take them in one stride, going one way and finish them off on the return journey. I suppose that to cut a whole tee with twelve foot gangs only took a couple of minutes.

Fairways were cut generally by me for the first few weeks of the new growing season, as I had ideas about shaping them; quite wrong, I have always thought, to have dead straight fairways all over the place, most uninteresting. A few gentle curves here and there make all the difference.

Then there was the semi-rough. A lot of courses don't bother with this item, but personally I think that to go from a nicely-mown fairway straight into rough grass is a bit tough on all concerned. So I used to mow round each fairway a mower's width just slightly higher than the actual fairway.

The rough of course is a subject for argument all over the golfing world; it depends really as to who owns the course in the first place. If the Members own the course then really in many ways it doesn't matter a hoot how high or rough the rough actually is, after all it's their rough and if they want to play that way, that's their privilege. *But* in this case I owned the place and I was dependant to a certain extent on the cash coming in from green fees or visitors. The average visitor merely wants a spot of fairly cheap exercise chasing a little white ball around a mile or two of nicely-mown grass. If he makes a muck-up of a drive (after all, quite a lot of us do), he doesn't want to spend hours looking for it (and the five minute rule is unknown to him). And what is a more and really important item on his agenda, is that he wants to finish his round in four hours or less and get back into the Club House with his mates, have a jar or three, some quick cooked unnourishing grub and back to the rat race which he avoided with possibly some guile in the morning. So the rough must be of a texture to penalise the hitter to some extent, but not give him the thought that he will never come near this damn course again.

I had five days of the week when I could share the place with visitors and Members, for the weekend was sacred for the Members and them alone. On the weekend the Member would arrive as early as 05.00 and pairs would tee off, depending on where they had booked on the list. That list would start off and go on throughout most of the day in eight minute intervals.

We tried four players all bashing a ball; that didn't work as it took hours for four people to get round the course and the people behind got frustrated. We tried four players and a couple of balls, that also was not so good and finally we hit on just two chaps hitting two balls and that's the way it went.

We tried ball chutes but the argument that arose as to whose ball belonged to who, gave me the willies and we stayed with the booking sheets.

It was very important as to when the new sheets for the next weekend went up on the board, they had to go up on the same day every week and also if possible at the same time.

I used to spend hours of hard-earned time in taking phone calls from Members in the early days, asking me to put their name down at a certain time on either the Saturday or the Sunday. I even went to the stage of buying one of those phones that don't have a cord which one can take round the house. I remember one day when I was enthroned on the seat of one of our small rooms, with the phone stuck in my pocket and it rang. The Member on the other end was most insistent that I drop anything that I was doing (I had done that from the trouser point of view), and rush, not proceed, but actually rush, to the said board and insert his name at 08.08 for the Saturday morning. That was the straw that broke my mental back and I told him with a slight rasp in my voice as to where I was at that precise moment, and if he wanted that time to tee off, then Mate, you come and make the mark yourself. After that my peristaltic action got back to normal.

It was about this time that I started the 'shotgun' Sunday and it was about the only way that you could get seventy-two players back into the Club House at more or less the same time. It went like this. Firstly there were seventy-two four ball players and they drew for lots firstly as to who they were going to play with, which was handy in that it mixed the Members up a bit and people played with other Members that they had seen in the car park or maybe hoisting a pint, but had never actually met. When you had seventy-two players all marked down, each four ball drew the hole from where he started, for instance if you drew hole four you finished on three and so on and so forth. You then got them all set up round the course, each tee with its four players waiting for the 'off' and the 'off', was the sound of my shotgun which I would fire on the highest part of the course. Then everybody would tee off and away they all went.

We went on to amalgamate the shotgun Sunday with an 'auction' dinner for the seventy-two drawn players the night before. This was good for the Club House coffers for seventy-two players at some £10.00 per head, and some wine thrown in for good measure, not only made a very merry evening but there was the added incentive that bets were then placed on the teams of each four concerned. I am uncertain as to whether the R&A really were all in favour of this sort of lark but it made the place swing. It also kept the financial wolf further from the door and Members could win quite a lot of boodle at the end of the day, always providing that they had backed the right four to win at favourable odds. It was also pleasant to see that when the list went up for who wanted to play in the auction/shotgun game, we were always well over subscribed and lots had to be drawn to see who would be playing and who would be watching from the sidelines.

So now, in my third year, with five hundred reasonably contented Members, I thought that a second man for the course would be appropriate and I advertised in the *Golfing World* for a man who wouldn't mind living in a tied cottage. It's not every worker who wants to be tied to the house that he lives in knowing that if he leaves the job, then come what may, he will have to leave the house as well. In all the many years that I was farming, and then latterly running a Golf Course and about 150 acres of farm land into the bargain, did I have any trouble about getting possession of a tied house when the man concerned left my employment. One or two dithered a bit for a week or two and one nearly came to court but normally there wasn't much bother.

In the farming world or profession, there is not so much of 'Master and Man', we generally all muck in together. In the past, before I got bogged down with paperwork, it was the done thing to go in for the local ploughing match. Often also included in the field was your own tractor driver, driving one of your tractors and plough, and if he beat the pants off you, so what. On the other hand, on the rare occasions when the decisions were reversed and you headed the match and got the cup there were one or two who didn't take kindly being beaten by the boss.

In those days it was the wife of the applicant who prodded her husband on to have a go for the post; she would like the village, there was a bus, she might even like the look of me. I used to get them both into the office and check what he knew about the job. It didn't take long to learn whether he was trying to fool you and merely wanted a job in the country after being out of work. Finally I would invite him out to one of the yards where I had prepared a tractor and trailer and ask him to join them up and back the lot through a gate — child's play for an experienced man but almost impossible for a beginner. And so, in this case, if he passed the test, you had a new man, and then you had to teach him a different ball game about working on his own on a Golf Course, which some of them didn't take kindly to at all.

If you don't play the game you never quite get the look of a green from, say a hundred yards away, you don't see the small faults that the last green keeper made when he mowed the day before yesterday, and so it was important that your workforce knew not only how to keep a course in good condition but how to play the game and if necessary enjoy it.

I used to get in touch with other Secretaries of other Golf Clubs and invite their staff to play ours when we thought that the place would be quiet. This did a lot of good from the staff point of view for the two sides used to chat professionally about the work concerned, and if I was playing as well, which I often did, sometimes it was an eye-opener to me as well as to what other courses did or didn't do. And then of course we would be invited back to the other Club and would play a round and would have the chance to see how the other half lived, so to speak.

It was a purely chance conversation in one of these staff matches when the other Secretary who was also playing asked me how I got on with Committees climbing all over me and having to do jobs which were downright stupid, all because the Chairman of the Green ordered you to do them. I put this Secretary in my particular picture and told him that when I had finished mowing the fairways I really didn't have much time to do much else bar eat and drink. He then understood that I owned the place and what was more was my own Secretary rolled into one. "Why don't you employ a Secretary?" says my golfing opponent for the day, striking one of those tricky approach shots between two bunkers and stopping the ball on the green within feet of the pin. My shot of course went straight into the nearest bunker.

So I started on the search for a Secretary. In my childlike ignorance I thought that what I knew by then about the care and maintenance of Golf Courses, he would regard it all as child's play and be able to teach me a thing or two about using tractors and mowing greens.

In the course of time and the with workload becoming greater and greater, I took on a charming chap who drove a Rolls, albeit somewhat old, and always arrived on five cylinders at about ten o'clock in the morning accompanied by two Siamese cats and a load of fish food. I always remember the first morning when he arrived minus the cylinder, stinking of fish and the cats purring all over the place. If I had had a hat on I would have doffed it, for a Rolls after all was the sign that you had arrived, arrived where is possibly a different story. I should have mentioned maybe that this chap was weekends only and he demanded and got a bedroom in our old manor house, right at the top of the house, where he used to make his early (or not so early) cup of tea and throw out the tea leaves over the window below which housed my sister-in-law. His cats had the habit of climbing up the curtains and in no time at all they were in tatters.

The final blow came when, without a great deal of thought, I asked him to mow the greens that particular morning as I had to go to the dentist. He went puce in the face with indignation and exclaimed that he was a Secretary of a Golf Club and as such was certainly not the sort of chap who would know the slightest thing about a mower, and after all what would the Members think if he was seen, perched on top of a mower doing such a menial task!

So he departed in high dudgeon to become a Secretary at another Golf Club and once again I started looking round for another chap who would help with the burden of running the mini empire which we seemed to be growing into. Membership had risen to some 600 plus, there was a new Ladies' Section and of course a Lady Captain which meant building separate showers and changing rooms and hanging pretty curtains on every window in sight, and most important, having a Ladies' morning where the male gender was not welcome on the course till later in the day.

On the subject of Captains, male, I had formed what came to be known as the Captain's Table, consisting of past Captains, the President, who was a personal friend of mine, the Secretary, if we had one at the time and myself. We used to meet once a year at a Dinner. There we would vote for the Captain for the next year, so that he would have a year as Vice-Captain to see what the job was all about, and if he was satisfactory he would be confirmed the following year.

It was laid down in the rules of the Club that the owner had the ultimate power of the veto, and in the fourteen years that I owned the place I only had to use it twice and once was for the choice of a Captain. The chap concerned, nice enough in many ways, was fond of the bottle and told me once that if ever he was made Captain of the Club he would make it his business to run me off the place. How exactly he was going to do this he never divulged. But when his particular name came down on a very short list I decided to edge him out of the running, so to speak, after all why invite trouble?

The other time was to do with the Handicap Committee. We found that we had got too many females on it and the men were in fact being outvoted and handicaps were being cut all over the place and mayhem was rearing its head. So for the last time I once again had to step in and see fair play.

The Members ran all their own Committees, such as Social Veterans and Match Committee, but I took on the business of new Members. I didn't want a Club consisting only of old school tie chaps, they can be somewhat tricky en-masse. I wanted a healthy mixture of twixt and between, which in the end I achieved and one had the odd barrister mixing with a taxi driver, all getting on fairly well together.

Each Member when elected was given a 'Father' for about three months. The Father would be a Member of at least two years or more standing and he would take on the new man and gradually show him everything about the Club and how it ran, and of course saw that he was always with a partner round the course. This worked quite well and some lasting friendships were made during the course of time.

We then, quite by accident, became keen on mucking about in boats. You see I had always had some sort of boat and whenever I had a spare moment I used to go out and fish or merely drop the hook somewhere quiet and go to sleep. Members got to hear about this and I was asked one day by a couple as to whether they could come out with me and try their hand at sea fishing. And back they came at the end of the day laden with fish of all shapes and sizes. The news spread to such an extent that I used to put up a list and charge £100 for twenty-four hours. This boat business which started in such an offbeat way, just with a couple who wanted the salt air on their skins, grew and grew and in the end was worth in the region of some £5,000 per year.

I had always been keen on boats. As a kid I used to muck about in sailing dinghies and they grew in size as I grew in years. The first real boat started its life as a lifeboat off a ship called the *Esperance Bay* and I bought the open boat complete with oars and all the rest. I laid in a dock, shoved a mast up and there was a nice thirty foot sloop. I found that I had to insert a centre plate as her so-called keels were no more than a few inches. I then bought a second-hand diesel and coupled that to a prop and there we were with quite a sound craft and vast compared with my previous little dinghies.

We wandered round the coast, my wife and I, and finally sailed up the Thames plus son and a friend of his. We were nearly thrown into the Tower of London because after passing under some bridge or other, there was the House of Commons in all its glory on our starboard side and I thought that it might be a fine place to moor up and admire all the scenery. No sooner had I thrown a rope round a convenient bollard, I was inundated with serious-looking policemen, who told us in no uncertain terms to "push off".

Our next spot of trouble was really my fault, for when I kitted the boat out with "heads" (loos) I forgot to tell any would-be passenger that the "head" on a boat is somewhat smaller than the one you find in a house. My son, Dear Boy, blocked the thing up solid and somewhere in the countryside of Surrey, we had to moor and unship the whole caboodle onto the bank watched by some curious passers-by. Once there, I had to use a long screwdriver to unblock the narrow pipe and then fit it all back again. *But* that was not quite the end of it because the bilges were full of "you know what" and had to be pumped dry, but still the stench prevailed, so I stole, while she was not looking, a somewhat costly bottle of Chanel belonging to my wife and that coupled with a few drops of concentrate Jeys fluid made the boat possible to live in.

I then sold wee *Esperance* and bought myself a proper seagoing craft, a Nicholson 38, which I moored down in Brighton Marina and it was on her that the Golf/Seagoing business really started. For the first couple who came out, more or less for free, told such glowing tales of their sailing day that I was besieged with people wanting to come for the weekend, quite forgetting that the Golf Course was reserved solely for Members on Saturday and Sunday. This was made even worse by the 'advert' or booking sheet that I posted which said "all found". What did I mean by all found, asked one, so I told him that I would provide all the food *and* the booze, and that was the meaning of "all found".

Now a Nicholson 38 has a cabin forward and a cabin aft, both with their own heads, and midships you had the dining/sitting area with the cockpit aft and all the navigating gear packed away neatly in the corner of the midships area. So I found, after some confusion when a lone female golfer found herself with three males and me, which didn't go down all that well, that I would only take married couples, and I would bunk down midships.

I increased the 'passage money' to £100 per person, per twenty-four hours, for everyone appeared to drink like fishes and empty gin and whisky bottles were seen sinking in our wake.

I told my would-be passengers that they must learn how to steer a boat such as this ketch, for unless we were moored somewhere I found it impossible to cook *and* man the wheel at the same time. This went down well and some of my paying 'crew' became quite proficient at handling three sails but the art of satellite navigation, with which I was equipped, was quite another kettle of fish and they all found this somewhat impossible to grasp.

I think, according to the letters of thanks that I received from many of my paying passengers, that they all enjoyed themselves doing something that some of them had probably dreamed about but had never been able to achieve. But the main thing, bar for giving pleasure to many people, was that the resulting income paid for my mooring fees and the residue, which was considerable, went back into the coffers of the growing Golf Club.

One day the phone went and a charming voice, with just the touch of the Irish sticking to it, said that he was a Golf Club Secretary, was fed up to the teeth with his present Club and had heard through the grapevine that I ran something quite unique in Golf Clubs in that the Members didn't run the place, I did. I agreed with all this and we met. I found him to be an ex-wing commander, DFC, who knew the rules of golf backwards; a subject I was weak on. He had never sat on a mower and wasn't all that keen to learn. But in this somewhat odd profession that I had found myself in, it was important that the man who was going to help me run the place was easy to get on with, and this chap was. I don't think we ever had a wry word in the two or three years that he was with me. I bought him a house nearby, only to find that his wife had run out on him and he was living with another man's property, which really was nothing to do with me, but there were some problems.

My President since we had started this caper had a breakdown and departed to the Midlands, so I had to find another. Golf Club Presidents are handy chaps to have around. They hand out prizes with a mixture of deference and surprise at the sight of the recipient, but always can be relied upon to murmur some well-chosen words of golfing lore.

The first President who we had for a very short space of time, resigned in high dudgeon as he was refused permission by a well-intentioned steward of the day to bring his Peke onto the course. The steward concerned unfortunately hadn't been told that although we didn't like dogs on the course, the President's dog was of course an exception.

My third and last President, unlike the first two, actually played the noble game and he was kind enough to let me take a ball or three of his from time to time, he was also one of the kindest chaps that I have had the pleasure to meet and had this happy knack of always giving you the impression that he really was glad to see one. We shared a liking for malt I seem to remember, and were at times caught by my better half having the one that we really came in for.

I haven't mentioned the subject of professional golfers, of whom we had our fair share, and of course at the start, not knowing anything concerned with golf, bar for playing it, I made my first of many 'muck-ups'. After the initial meeting in the Village Hall, where it was decided that come what may we would build ourselves a Golf Course, I was rung up by a very well-known professional golfer who asked me as to whether I wanted a Pro. I said I hadn't thought much about the matter but if he wanted to come in at the start, then he was more than welcome. I didn't give the impression that everything depended on whether this man took the post, in fact with one thing and another, I wasn't all that interested in professional golfers.

I was somewhat taken aback a few weeks later when again the phone rang and a voice said that he was the agent for this Pro and he would want £1,000 per year as a retainer, to let the Pro come and set up shop at my Club. Although at this time money was flowing in quite fast, it was also going out at a much more rapid rate and this sudden demand for £1,000 rather rubbed me up the wrong way and I told the man concerned in the politest way possible what he could do with his demand and for that matter with his Pro.

Then in the course of time another well-known Pro got in touch and he asked for the job, wanted a retainer and a percentage of the green fees, he also wanted free light, free phone calls and free heating. We struck a bargain in that I would in fact pay him a retainer and a percentage of the green fees and supply wood for the then wood-burning stove that I had in his future shop, but he would have to light it.

And so for a while this arrangement worked quite well bar for the fact that as I was an early riser and was quite often about the place at 05.00, I refused to give the Pro any percentage of the green fees that I personally took before he surfaced at about 08.30. After all if he couldn't get up or get his staff up then he couldn't be all that hungry for cash. There came the time also when I was very short of cash and decided that rightly or wrongly I was no longer going to pay the Pro this retainer for being self-employed, after all I argued with myself I was self-employed and nobody had thought to pay me a retainer. So after some discussion I terminated his contract and there and then invited him to continue with a fresh one, without of course the retainer.

All hell broke out then and the Secretary of the PGA (Professional Golfers Association) came down and banged his own particular drum about how I should treat his member. I confess that we had somewhat of a stand-up row and agreed to differ on this particular point and also on the hardy old perennial that according to PGA rules no professional should undercut another's prices for such items as golf equipment. This seemed to be such a stupid idea and I told him so with or without the proverbial shovel, even offered to take the shop over and put the present Pro in as seller of equipment, pay him a decent salary and take the rest of the profit, if any, for myself. But this suggestion so inflamed the gentleman that he stormed out in a cloud of blue smoke.

In the end my Pro stayed with me without a retainer but with a nice fat fee coming in from the percentage of the green fees, and although I say it myself, we got on quite well together and I was fortunate enough to be able to help him in some family matters that were causing some concern.

On the subject of the Pro's wood stove, we had mainly, because I had some twenty acres of woods, quite a bit of free fire wood, and in two of the ex-farm cottages I had installed wood cookers that not only cooked a decent roast but also heated up to five radiators and the necessary hot water into the bargain. Then of course there was Horace in the Club House, not forgetting Henrietta, his mate. Horace was one of these Norwegian wood stoves that threw off thousands of BTUs and he was installed in the Club House. He really did a good job and warmed the backsides of countless golfers.

C

Whereas Henrietta was of enormous proportions and would with no trouble whatsoever take a bale of straw into her cavernous maw, let alone four-foot logs, and it was she who heated the Club House radiators and provided hot water for washing and showers for cold bodies, etc., etc. Henrietta was also fairly clever in that she could, at the turn of a switch, sort her insides to work on oil, so that if we were rushed on the course and couldn't spare the one day for sawing wood up in the minute forest, then she would still provide enough heat for all and sundry.

The day we chose for gathering in trailer-loads of wood was not all that simple in that we had to actually fell trees, cut off the top and lop as it's called and then get down to sawing off logs for Horace at one length, for Henrietta at another, for the Pro's shop, that had a very small wood burner, a mere foot was enough for that and for the various farm cottages, where the wife would demand a certain type of wood that would create quick heat for a chop but would also want a slow-burning wood for baking the bread. All this wood, sawn into the correct lengths, had to be housed; not the slightest use in going to all the trouble and sweat to saw up a log then let the rain beat down on it.

Having worked for some two hard years as a lumberjack in my youth in Australia before the war it soon became quite clear that none of the staff knew the slightest thing about felling a tree and plonking it down within a few feet of the designated site. So I found that I had to teach this gentle art from the roots up, so to speak, no easy task but I am glad to say that we didn't drop a tree on anyone's head although there were some narrow squeaks.

So one day of the week was spent up in the woods and the noise of the chain saw and the ring of axes would sound throughout our long valleys as trees came crashing down, and with the help of a mounted circular saw, logs of all shapes and sizes were produced. We used to try and get a trailer-load to each cottage. There were three of them, one to Henrietta, another to Horace and anything left over used to tumble down my own cellar at the end of the long day.

In the early days with little help, I used to have to break off from cutting wood to go and man the bar, for the evening trade was at time quite brisk. I had purchased a snooker table which was popular and one of the old barns was turned into a badminton court, so by 9 p.m. when I firmly shut up shop, I had had enough for the day.

New Members were still coming in thick and fast. What they liked about the place I never knew, maybe it was because at one moment they were asking to be a Member, the next moment I would ask them if they had their cheque book. If they had, then in a jiffy they were in, no fuss, no Committees deciding that they hadn't gone to the right school or that we weren't interested in plumbers becoming Members.

On the other hand, the chap who would turn up and say that he had *never* played the game at all but thought he ought to start and what did I suggest? I used to adopt another ploy with him, he would become a Temporary Member, pay his full fees but was *not* allowed on the course till he obtained, what I used to call, a Club Handicap. If he didn't obtain one in a certain length of time, then he could either become a Social Member or he could leave and go somewhere else and I would give him something back from his original fee that he had paid. But this seldom happened, if the man or woman for that matter was keen enough to join a Golf Club, then they were keen enough to obtain this private handicap.

The Pros were keen on the idea, for the man concerned was handed over to them and they were let loose on our somewhat large practice ground. In the early days, we had three rough holes made and the pupils had to go round these holes in a certain number of shots and also extract themselves out of the man-sized bunker we had constructed. When they had done all this, they were allotted a 'Father' and turned loose on the main course. I should have added they also were questioned about the rules of golf as laid down by the R&A. Generally, depending on the weather, the fledgling Member would become fully-fledged in three months or less and it was thought by Members to be an asset to the Club as a whole.

When the Club was about three years 'young' we acquired a man who was master of no particular trade but could turn his hand to anything on a farm, or for that matter a Golf Course. He could plumb, carpenter, plaster, put in a ring main, sharpen a circular saw and after a while, because I taught him, he became quite a dab hand at welding. He loathed golf and refused point blank to learn and although he could drive a tractor he was not all that keen, but he was worth his weight in gold for the number of jobs that came up to do in our little mini empire were legion. He was never off sick and I think that I can say that he was never late for work. He had nothing to do with the course as such but was always found to be doing something, whether it was fencing, mending the automatic sprinkling water set-up that we had round each green and on most tees, to finding out why a certain mower would never want to start when its engine was warm.

Of course his first job of the day was to tend to the needs of Henrietta and Horace. The former would have been banked up the night before, always providing that the steward on duty at the bar (when we had one) remembered to do the job. If the steward had forgotten then of course she would have to be lit from cold and it would be an hour or so before there was a hot water supply or any of the radiators become hot. Horace was easier. There was always a large amount of dried wood surrounding him. Open the flue and shove in a couple of logs and away he would go, giving out a nice warmth within twenty feet or so.

My first job of the day in summer was to go round the course to see whether all the greens were in the same place, for very occasionally vandals would appear in the night, take a liking to a few flags and tee boxes and these would need to be replaced. I used to walk or jog the course but I found in time that with advancing years this was not on, so I bought myself a very small Honda motorbike which used to swarm up some of our steeper slopes with great ease and the two dogs, one a Dane the other a Doberman having to put their

36

paws forward to keep up the pace.

Sometimes there would be a baying from the Doberman who would find somebody who shouldn't be there and I would go and investigate. At times one would catch a chap actually hauling something off the course down to a waiting car or van and backed up with a nine stone Dane and a slavering Doberman, the argument, if any, would be brief. Other times you would find a 'biking' golfer who said that he couldn't find anyone to pay his green fee to, so thought he would pay when he had finished. These types would park their car in some handy gateway leading on to the course, leap nimbly over the gate armed with clubs and calmly start playing but never of course within sight of the Club House or any normal civilisation. I used to demand and get double the normal green fee and watch with some satisfaction as his next shot slammed into a ruddy great bunker, a sure sign that he felt rattled.

Having done the round of the course, checked that the sprinklers had worked during the night, if they had been programmed to turn on, I would then return to the green keeper's hut and write up the report. This might consist of the following: no 2 green had now five weeds; no 8 sprinkler was on the blink and had watered everything bar the green and the flag of no 8 had been pinched. Once a week I would also poke into each green a monitor to show lack or surplus of lime or potash, etc., etc., and again this would go down in the log. The head green keeper and his mate would on pay day present a diary of their week's work and it was a simple task to check that what I had put down in the log had actually been done.

Back to breakfast at about 08.00 and go through the mail. Bills to pay on one side and receipts, etc., on the other and in the early days when cows were still about, I would get one of the children, then ten and eight, to phone up the AI for Buttercup to be 'done'. At about 11.00 a chap would call, Buttercup would be ushered in, a tube would be inserted into the right orifice and with any luck in nine months time, Buttercup would deliver up a calf. It was a simple way to teach your children the so-called fable of the birds and the bees.

After breakfast or sometimes before, depending on the time factor I would go down to the Club House, argue with the burglar alarm, nip in before it went off, and zero it for the day. Then the till roll from the previous day, always an interesting job for the till was one of those clever machines that would break down into columns what you had sold during the last twenty-four hours; how much for beer, how much for food, wine, spirits, even the odd green fee from someone who had found the Pro's shop shut and me away somewhere on the course, so had come to the bar to pay his dues. Knowing what the float was day by day one then had to subtract that from the total rung up on the till to see how close the steward was. Having done the job myself for more time that I like to remember, I would never blame him or her if they were a few bob out. I used to take a daily check on what spirits there were and put a spare bottle out from the cellar should it be necessary.

Then there was the one-armed bandit that had to be sorted out and this was quite a job on its own. For the large sum of 10p the player could win, and once a fortnight he did, £200 in 50p pieces, which would cascade down a chute. If this happened on a weekend when the bar was crowded, the winner was expected to pay for drinks all round which made a bit of a dent in his winnings but the more people who actually saw the machine gush out this amount, the better, it was good advertising. But from my point of view in the early hours, the story was a bit different. I had to fill up the various tubes that held the money that *could* be won, also if I was in luck clear out the box that held the overflow of 10p bits and mark it up in the ledger. It was more than pleasant if there hadn't been a big winner the day before, then my cash box would be laden with boodle but if the reverse was the case then the inserted cash would merely go into the various tubes till they were filled.

Once in a while you had a problem with cash and booze. It went like this. I would know by experience how much spirits had been sold, not only by the till mark-up but merely by looking at the bottles on the rack, and week by week I found that I was a bottle of Scotch out, not every same day but once a week a bottle would go missing. By this time I knew pretty well all the ways that a barman who was a bit bent could do you, but this man was as straight as a die, I would have bet on it. So I started working out who actually had access to the bar area. There was the cook but she regarded drink as something wicked and wouldn't even enter the bar; as far as she was concerned that part of the Club House had a rotten smell, no it couldn't be her. Then there was the cleaner. She was the wife of one of the green keepers, but she was such a kind soul and personally I felt sorry for her, for her husband was alleged to be a bit of a drunk, and was thought to knock her about a bit. She was so thoughtful about my property too. I remember that we had to buy a new Hoover as the old one had given up the ghost and when the new machine arrived I can well recall how she thought that she ought to take this Hoover back home every night just in case it got pinched. That sort of thoughtfulness on the part of my staff made my day. But one day quite by accident I passed her on the way home with the Hoover clutched to her ample chest, and I stopped her to say something or other and suggested that she put the machine down as it must be heavy for her, she did and it clinked. Now I don't pretend that I am all that bright but as I was talking to her and saying how nice the Club House looked, the back end of what brain I have was churning away regarding this sudden clinking sound. All of a sudden I barked "Open that Hoover up" and there, not well padded, was a 40oz bottle of Scotch with my label on it. I then had to find not only another green keeper but a cleaning lady into the bargain.

It was around about this time, when things generally were going well, 700 Members were paying their just dues, the bar was rattling in the lolly and the one-armed chap was going berserk. Societies were coming and going and quite a few were booking for the following year. Then someone from one of these Societies left a lighted fag end down the backside of our costly £5.00 arm chairs and the whole Club House went up in smoke.

It all happened like this. Not that it matters or pertains to the story but I like to sleep in the nether nether, if you take my drift and at about 02.00 I was awakened from my first deep slumber by the frantic hooting of a horn outside the window. Leaping up without much of a thought I dashed to the curtains and drew them back, thus exposing my all to the startled gaze of the wife of the bar steward who lived in the flat by the Club House. Modestly averting her eyesight she yelled from the car that the Club House was well alight and would I perhaps ring 999. By that time I had put my teeth in, draped a pair of trousers round the bottom half and an old sweater round the top. The first fire appliance was sweeping into the car park, timing its arrival, and mine for that matter, as the roof caved in with a roar. The second and then the third appliance arrived (for some reason or other, it is not the done thing to call them fire engines) and hoses were snaking all about the place.

The first snag in all this occurred quite soon when the first arrival ran out of water and demanded to know where the fire hydrant happened to be situated. They carry, it would appear, some four hundred gallons which is fine to douse the odd chimney fire but not something like this. Having lived in the place for twenty-seven years I felt a bit of a twit when I said that really I hadn't a clue, but suddenly a brilliant idea flitted across my mind in that under our very feet was an underground tank into which all the car park water drained. And so eager hoses flashed down into the underground depths of this quite large catchment, but what I had forgotten in the excitement was the fact that when I was farming, the results of the back end of countless cows was also washed down into this same area. Very soon instead of a nice clear jet of water there appeared a dirty brown one which when it hit the still smouldering remains of our Club House emitted a stench which appeared to cover half of Kent. At this stage two past Captains of the Club appeared on the scene and I found myself in the middle of a small Committee meeting but declined at that stage to embark on the chore of taking minutes. By about 05.00 the worst was over, the fire chaps were coiling up their somewhat smelly hoses, billy cans appeared and tea was brewed up on the remains of our quite nice Club House.

I then retired having I felt earned a decent cooked breakfast, only to the called to the phone by a chap who described himself as a fire assessor who said that he had just heard about my sad loss (one wonders as to how the news had reached him) and made it quite plain that I shouldn't stir a step till we had had a chat. Being of a somewhat cautious disposition, especially at that time in the morning, I said that I was going to finish my breakfast first come what may. But before I had been able to take another bite, the back door pealed and there was another assessor trying to get in fast as my Dane had taken a liking to his pants and what they contained. I took the Dane in and shoved him out and finished my somewhat cold breakfast, with my mind whirling around as to what to do first.

I went down to the sodden and blackened car park to find three assessors regarding each other with some dislike and was able to carry out a sort of Dutch auction, first going to one and asking his lowest quote, and then trotting over to the next and asking him as to whether he could beat this particular price, and in this fashion I was able to get the percentage down to 3% which saved me some £2,000.

At this time we were dabbling with people called 'franchise holders'. This particular lot were a nice family, slightly scatterbrained if they don't mind me mentioning it, for in their contract was the necessity of insuring their part of the business of running the Club House, in particular loss of profits.

We had tried all sorts of systems regarding the running of the Golf Club House. We started as I think I have told you with my long-suffering wife in the cook house, coping with school runs and cooking for hundreds of people, with me in the bar and when the bar was closed, dashing off to cut greens. The pace couldn't last and the next stage was one of the happiest in my life. My son Richard had always from the cradle up stated quite clearly that he was going into catering and possibly buy a hotel or two. As luck would have it he had just successfully completed his three-year course at Westminster Tech and thought that he ought to get a bit of commercial practice in. So he came and took over the cook house and the Members got fat and quite satisfied. I for good measure at the same time gave up doing the bar which was a bit of a tie in more ways than one. Richard did us proud for three very happy years and he then went out and found himself a wife and a pub, more or less in that order and as I write this, he has bought the pub concerned, which is in Mayfield, his food is sixth in England according to Mr Ronnay, he has three quite lovely daughters and appears to be set for a more than contented life.

We then tried all manner of different ways of running the Club House. When desperate we employed a well-know team of caterers to take over the lot and in six months we lost £5,000.

We then tried employing a man for the bar and giving the cook house for free to the wife, less the gas she used. That would work quite well for a time, the wife would make lots of lolly cooking for vast numbers of Members. But she would then find that if she employed someone else to do the cooking, then she could get out and see the distant bright lights. This wouldn't go down at all well with the husband who was left behind to run the bar, and from the Member's point of view the quality of food dropped like a stone and there were complaints all round. The inevitable day came when one would have to have a fairly gentle word with the wife, who would then take 'um' backed up by her husband and quick as a flash they would be off, quite often to another Golf Club. Generally it wasn't the 'done' thing for one Golf Club to hijack another's staff, but if they were desperate, then they would, only after a while ringing up and asking as to whether I knew a Mr and Mrs X. If I said I knew them only too well and not to touch them with a long barge pole, there was a slight silence the other end.

Normally Secretaries of Golf Clubs had a fairly well defined line of somewhat classified information between themselves. It used to work well with the Societies, for if a Secretary of a Golfing Society rang up and wanted to book a day for fifty bodies, starting with coffee, golf, lunch, more golf and then possibly dinner, then the Club concerned was in those days looking at £100 per head plus, *but* what were they like? So you asked the Secretary, just as a matter of interest, one didn't want to look as if one was prying, where else they had played in this particular county. If he hedged, then with regrets, any date he wanted, wasn't available. *But* if he gave the name of a Club, it didn't really matter whether it was nudging John o' Groat's, it had to have a Secretary who you could ring up and ask what did he think of XYZ Golfing Society. Then you got the truth, the whole truth and no holes barred. Some were meticulous in their manners towards the course and Club House, others were out and out sods of the first water.

The old boy network was also handy regarding new Members who would ring up, book an interview, and ask to become Members. "Have you been a Member of a Golf Club before?"

"Yes" said the applicant who then gave the necessary information.

I would then ring up the Secretary of the Club concerned. If he said "You can have him and the best of British luck" or words to that effect, the chap concerned would find when he returned, that with the greatest of regrets his particular handicap niche was full for the moment.

But to return to my blackened and twisted remains of a once very comfortable Club House. The time of day was about 10.00 and I rang my brewers and explained the situation and said I wanted beer, glasses and a few other oddments. They didn't want to know. I was small fry and not really worth the bother. So I then phoned a family brewing company in Kent and they, bless their hearts, turned up trumps and delivered all I wanted, merely on my word that I wouldn't deal in future with anyone else. To this I agreed subject to the problem that if they had a strike then I would have to get my supplies from somewhere else.

I called in all the staff, that sounds very grand, it could mean that hoards of green keepers came trotting along off the course, but we only had two but they really pulled their weight. We had an old barn not doing much, and that very afternoon the staff shot up into the woods, cut down sufficient poles to create a false ceiling, covered that with some green netting that we just happened to have around saved from farming days, and there we were with a very rough and somewhat ready temporary Club House ready to open for trade that very night. I should add maybe that the Secretary that I had was due to leave this very day which didn't altogether help but he had his problems and I got on with mine.

The day hadn't finished by any means. I rearranged the franchise couple who had lost their job on a temporary basis and rang up three builders. The first was due to arrive the next tomorrow morning so as to get on with the rebuilding of a new Club House.

I had of course told my insurance company the bad news and they were kind enough to say that I could get on with the job subject to price. I learnt a lot from this fire. I made a number of mistakes, such as forgetting to insure telephones, electric meters, the one-armed bandit and the big one was regarding the loss of profits. Owing to the fact that I had got the ball rolling rather rapidly, in that the Club House was a smouldering wreck at 5.00 in the morning, yet I was able to carry on business that same evening, my insurance company were not prepared to pay out a penny bit on this clause, but in the end they did actually cough up a small proportion of what it might have been *if* I had just waited till the new building was finished. By that time I would no doubt have lost a number of Members who quite rightly expect a place to drink their beer and have their food.

That evening there was quite a party in our new Barn/Club House. The Members liked the rustic feeling of the place and they turned up in their hundreds to view the wreck and to see what I had been up to, to make all this possible. They were more than kind, in fact they prodded me into making a statement/speech, call it what you will. Our President, who just happened to be present, replied and altogether it was quite an evening.

As I locked up that night, stepped out into what was still a stinking mess of blackened twisted timbers, a fox or it could have been a dog was seen cocking its leg against a tall fallen rafter, no doubt leaving its own particular message for all of its kind to sniff.

To people who live in the country, we know, or we think we know why a dog lifts a leg. It goes like this:

> *The dogs once called a meeting,*
> *They came from near and far,*
> *Some came by aeroplane*
> *And some by motor car.*
>
> *But before into the meeting house,*
> *They were allowed to look,*
> *They had to take their bottoms off,*
> *And hang them on a hook.*
>
> *No sooner were they seated,*
> *Each mother's son and sire,*
> *When a nasty little yellow dog,*
> *Rushed in and shouted 'FIRE'.*
>
> *They all got up in frantic haste,*
> *They hadn't time to look,*
> *And each seized at random,*
> *A bottom from a hook.*
>
> *They got their bottoms all mixed up,*
> *It made them very sore,*
> *To have to wear a bottom,*
> *That they'd never worn before.*

So that is why today, you see,
A dog will even leave a bone,
To smell another's bottom,
In the hope to find his own.

And so this day ended, we had started with a Club House, now we were without one, we had a Secretary but his notice was up and he had left. We had lost two franchise holders and they in turn had sacked their two and only staff, but I had taken them on again on a temporary basis. We had lost our original brewers, but had found a nice family one, fire assessors had come and gone and tomorrow was another day with one builder in the morning and another in the afternoon.

I slept deeply and I am told by my wife that I twitched all through the small hours. The next day arrived as days do and the first builder started to talk way over my financial head from the point of view of cost. We had some £65,000 to play with for the building itself and a bit more for the contents but I had to tread with some caution. I plied him with a gin or three and he departed and I waited for the second builder to turn up after lunch.

I remember during the morning, the Lady Captain wanted to see me regarding her Lady Members and the thought that should they want to spend a proverbial penny whilst in our rustic barn they had to trot quite a way with their legs crossed and could I do something about it. Now we had a hut of sorts that was stuck up on our high part of the course. There the wind, when it wanted to whine, really went to London Town and Members who huddled in it would have a quick drag on a fag and decide that this was the spot where they really ought to have a new ball so then dropped the wrapper on the earth floor. A courting couple were even found in the depths of winter with the lady looking discontented as the Member in question, who must with deep regret be nameless, had problems with the arctic cold temperatures and should really have come armed with a blowtorch. So we took it to bits and shoved it next door to our new rustic Club House with a

46

thunder bin, bolted down onto some sleepers, for the use of Lady Members.

After we had been going for about a week (our handyman had even built a huge fireplace), we had problems in the shape of the local law who had arrived around about 12.00 and asked to see me. "You are aware Sir, that you are breaking the law by selling drink in these premises."

"No" I said, "I have a licence from the Bench to sell liquor."

"In the old Club House, you had."

"But it's only a few yards away" says I. And that was really the point, a few yards made all the difference. So I asked our local law, who was a nice chap and played golf off and on with us, as to whether it would be OK if I gave the stuff away in this rustic bar.

"Oh yes, Sir, that would be within the law, nothing against giving the stuff away."

So whilst he was in the bar, sipping a jar or two, I made out a notice for all to see which read roughly as follows: *The drink in this bar is FREE. But should you wish to donate any small gift to the Club, then the following might fit our particular problem.* And after that I listed the bar prices. "How's that" I asked our friendly policeman.

"Very neat, Sir" says he and finished his pint, wished us well and he and panda departed.

We had one or two clever chaps who insisted in not donating anything to this particular charity, but in the main, the Members understood and anyway they were very happy with what had been done for their particular comfort.

I engaged a firm to build me a new Club House and out of the ashes of the old came a new modern building, better built than the old but not quite the home from home that the old one had been. It didn't have the smoky atmosphere, and we had lost things that we couldn't really replace, like the Hole-in-One Board with all the names of King Holers marked up in golden letters. The Lonely Hearts Board, that went too. On it went the names and phone numbers of men who wanted a game on a certain day and time and other people would come along and ring them up to arrange a game; it proved a very popular idea.

After about some six months we shifted out of our more than popular barn of a Club House. I had after all obtained a licence to sell drink so I had to go to court again to get the licence shifted some fifty yards to the new building. We had quite a day when we finally secured the keys. All the Members, who by that time were just over 700, were told and the place was packed, maybe because the news had got round that the first drink was on the house.

And so things went on in their own sweet way. Members came fishing most weeks with me; in the end I had to put a list up as numbers were getting more than I or for that matter the boat could cope with. The shooting on the rest of the farm and woodlands also went well and I even found time to teach a few interested golfers the more gentle art of casting a fly on a small pond that I had found, or to be more accurate a stick that I used to use for discovering where underground streams ran had found.

I found, quite by accident, a new Secretary who I had known for years who used to run another Club nearby. One day he rang up and said that he was fed-up to the teeth where he was as he always seemed to be at the beck and call of countless Committees. If he came to see me, what would be the drill? he asked. I told him that with me it was quite the other way around, in that the Committees at our Club had a free hand in running their own affairs, but all minutes of every meeting had to be countersigned by the Secretary, and if the Secretary was absent by me. He was with me for three very happy years; we never even had a written contract between us. He died of cancer of the throat. I saw him on the day he went, for I used to pop in and shave his wasted face and tell silly stories, which I don't think he could even hear let alone understand. I am not ashamed to say that for days after I wasn't really dry-eyed and the place wasn't the same without him.

I got another Secretary who actually was a Member, but before I took him on I told him that I wanted him to be able to set a mower down to three sixteenths to mow a green and learn how to cut the fairways, change a hole and cut a hedge. When he had mastered all that, I showed him around a bar and taught him how to pull a pint, how to treat the customers, how to make Members feel that they are wanted, how to be able to keep three bars going on his own and how to clean the beer pipes and so on. Finally I prodded the Pro into taking him into his shop for a week to see what went on behind the scenes. Lastly he came to the office, this part was easier as he was a trained accountant and here he was able to put my somewhat ancient bookkeeping into a better state for all concerned.

You see I have this bee in my bonnet that if you are going to be in business and the Golf Club was quite big business by that time (I was making enough money to be able to invest it for the first time in my life), one should know when any one of your staff is making a muck-up of this or that and be able to put them right. They, the staff, will respect you a lot more *if* you are able to do their jobs as well as they can.

I gradually found that I was working myself out of a job, the Secretary was efficient, the staff were happy and even the Club House staff appeared to be staying, for at the best of times they are apt to be a bit nomadic. I cannot say I blame them, boredom and long hours, coupled with the fact that some of our Members had the habit of treating them as mere servants. I have at times been in the Club House drinking a reflective pint and one of these rude types would come in, stride to the bar, bang on the counter and say "Pint." No "Good Morning." No "Please" and the very idea of saying "Thank You" never entered his head. I would, if I was quick enough to catch the steward's eye, shake my head and the steward would understand and wander off leaving the Member puce in the face with rage.

I used to then wander round the serving side myself and say quite gently to the Member "Why not try that again." It only took a few minutes but he learnt that nice old Winchester saying 'That manners maketh man'.

D

It was the sudden understanding that I really couldn't have cared less whether this mannerless man left the Club or not which prodded me into the next big activity in my life, which was to sell-up and get out and leave all the worry and hassle to someone else. I was sixty-four years young and felt that I had a bit left in me. So slowly but surely I lulled myself into the feeling that tomorrow I would be free, no longer would I have to be pleasant to people who really couldn't care less as to whether I was polite or not, we, my charming better half and I, could relax and enjoy the autumn of our respective lives.

But it wasn't going to be all that easy I thought. It seemed the proper thing to do was to offer the whole place to the Members first. Of course the whole place had grown somewhat since we started. We began with an old Manor House and one cottage and a barn or two, and here we were with still the Manor House, but three cottages, a thriving Club House, an eighteen hole Golf Club and another hundred acres to boot.

So I called a meeting, well advertised in advance, and out of the 700 Members that we had at the time, some sixty or so turned up, and I put it to them. I said that I wasn't as young as I used to be, that I wanted a bit of peace and I was going to sell. Would they like to own the lot? I left the meeting with the promise that I would come back in half-an-hour when they had had a natter between themselves. In due time I was called back to the meeting, given a beer and was told that they would in fact like to buy the place. "What might you be offering?" said I.

"We can raise £20,000" said the chairman of the meeting.

I wasn't certain as to whether they had got the whole thing right in their respective minds. For they were offering in all sincerity, £20,000 for a seven-bedroom Manor House, three four-bedroom cottages, 140 acres of Golf Course plus another 100 acres plus of farm land, all the goodwill (and there was quite a bit of that) and all the dead stock (which amounted to, at the last insurance valuation, some £35,000 plus). So I, looking I hope most sad, turned their offer down.

Then the press got hold of the news and for weeks I was

50

badgered by worthy buyers, who said that they would love to live in the Manor House but were not really interested in anything else, or another who wanted just one four-bedroom cottage, but wasn't interested in the rest.

Then quite out of the blue, a Member, who generally played about once or twice a year rang up and said he wanted to buy the place, not just the Manor House, not just the cottages, but the whole 'shebang'. He brought along his solicitors, accountants, and I went through the somewhat long motion of debriefing myself of the twenty-seven years that we had had the farm and the fourteen years or so that we had built and owned the Golf Course — it took days.

I was particular in that he should keep my staff, they had been pretty good to me throughout the years, and to this the would-be purchaser agreed.

He wanted a complete inventory of everything I had, and I confess that together with most farmers, I was apt to hang on to things that I really knew I would never use. I had countless spare parts for ploughs, medicine for cows that went to market years ago, little red rubber rings which were used for castrating ram lambs, spare parts for combines, you name it, I had it.

The staff and I collected everything we had into one long barn and I looked at it and thought that I would never be able to put all this down in type, so I got my tape recorder. It was the one I used to use in the early hours of the morning when I went round the course (I would natter into the mike and leave it all in the head green keeper's shed so that he could have a first-hand account for that particular day of what needed doing). I went from item to item in this barn and I would switch the set on and say "Loos one, for the use of — Plough point ten inch" and so on and so forth. When I had finished the lot I sent the whole tape, full on both sides, to their solicitor. He didn't exactly like this method, but I had done my part, he had everything I owned down and all he had to do was to get some fast typist to shove it all down on a bit of paper.

Everything appeared to be going along fine, so my wife and I, who seldom used to take a holiday, decided that we deserved one. I hired a little house in France in the sun and on a nice sandy beach and proceeded for one glorious week to do nothing but lie in the sun.

At the end of this week, my Secretary rang up and said the deal was off as the buyer had changed his mind. So that was the end of that, we came back right away and I put the whole place into the hands of estate agents. Once again people came along and measured this and that, took pretty pictures and finally presented me with a costly-bound volume of what was for sale.

All this took about a month and one day the phone went and the potential buyer who had cut short my holiday at a stroke, came on and said he had changed his mind and now once again wanted to buy the whole place. I wasn't prepared to go behind the backs of the estate agents who now had the place firmly in hand so I told my buyer that he would have to deal with the agents, and what was more that it would now cost him thousands more through commission that the agents would quite rightly charge. All this didn't seem to change his mind and he offered me a figure plus the commission and I accepted then and there. A day or two later he paid over his deposit.

Whilst all this was going on, we had for months been looking for a place to rest our heads; four bedrooms and a sitting room would be handy, and possibly a dinning room thrown in for good measure, plus of course a bath or two and the things that go with bathrooms, and we wanted it near to the sea or on a river. For months we had been inundated with houses containing more bedrooms than the old Manor House or we would be given a cottage in the wilds of Dartmouth with one bedroom and an outside loo. We travelled miles looking at quite ghastly places, some we would take one look at and decide that this was not for us. I was the one who had to go up the garden path and knock on the door and say how sorry we were, but — I got dirty looks at times.

In the end, with completion day looming for everything bar the Manor House, we found our present abode and on

August 1st 1983, I signed away some twenty-seven years of our farming and golfing life, and we were due to vacate the house on about August 15th.

I got several quotes to shift us from Kent to Sussex by the sea and although Pickfords were not the cheapest, they certainly did us proud; everything packed away with mountains of newspaper in eighty-three tea chests, our clothes on their own hangers, straight into their vast vans, all covered up, the same with my wife's dresses. They took two days to pack us up; every drawer emptied and every stick of furniture colour marked by my efficient wife. She had also taken the precaution of marking the doors of our new house, so that all Pickfords had to do when they and their four vans arrived was to match the colour sticker on the furniture to the colour on the door. It seemed so simple. Something just had to go wrong. And it did.

Our last night in the old Manor was spent in one bed, two deck chairs, a bottle of something and two throw-away paper mugs, everything else was packed and outside in their four locked vans. Now we had two cars, my wife wedded to her Mini and I had a Saab. I always kept all my keys, including my car and house keys on a chain which was fastened to my belt and ended up in my pocket. My wife always without fail, as soon as she came into the house would open a certain kitchen drawer and place her keys inside. The Pickfords men arrived at sparrows fart, up with the bed and the deck chairs, into the last van and waved a cheery farewell with me saying that we would meet them at the front door of our new house.

That was fine so far bar for the fact that Minis, like a lot of other cars, need ignition keys and our lot was speeding through our narrow Kent lanes and heading for points South.

No time to fiddle with bits of wire to circumvent the ignition key. I shot down to the garage where we had bought the car in the first place with the number of the key, which as luck would have it I had on a disc on my chain and obtained a spare key. Back to the house and off we went chasing four large vans which had at least half-an-hour's start on us. I in the Saab, with the keys of the new house in my pocket, shot off with the turbo charger whining in protest and passed the four vans just a few miles from our new front door. In due course the Mini arrived with worried-looking wife to be assured by Mr Pickford that everything was going into the right room. They, the Pickford men, would have willingly unpacked for us but we felt that we would then spend weeks finding out just where they had put this and that, so we settled down in the kitchen and started unwrapping all the countless items that we had amassed over the years and stowing them all away where we thought best.

So here we are, in the autumn of our lives, in a nice house, maybe it's a bit big but for twenty-seven years we had lived in a big house with vast cellars, and old habits die hard. Nobody can build in front of us for the sea comes up, sometimes in a friendly fashion, sometimes quite the reverse, to within a few feet of our garden wall. Behind us is the Golf Course where the powers that be have kindly allowed me to become a Member and I struggle at times with the continual southwest winds to keep within my handicap of 18. I have my boat *L'Autre Femme* down at Brighton and every Saturday I am let off the lead and allowed to go and talk to her, clean her up, polish her topside not forgetting her bottom, and at times when the weather is right, we go out, she and I holding hands, so to speak, for I have had a certain nice relationship with boats, both big and small for more years than I care to remember. We seem to understand each other, I treat her with some respect and certainly the element that surrounds her, here I doff my nautical cap for the sea can never, like a bull, be trusted.

I play golf about three days a week with people that I can now call friends. I have found that you need a calculator to count your acquaintances but friends, now that's a different kettle of fish. With me, I find that being with a man, without uttering a word for minutes or even hours and without feeling that you *had* to, means that somehow or other one is on the same wavelength and you are both at peace with your own thoughts. I confess that I have never quite had the same feeling with a female. I find myself eyeing her figure and wondering what's hidden under all the garments and thinking possibly of bed and all that, but then 'all that' would hurt someone, and anyway I am more than content.

As a new Member at the Golf Club I find myself at continual pains to hold my thoughts in check, for I can see all their problems, and I can see most of the answers. Their profit is counted almost in pence per year and yet there is a continual cry for more money. Their mistakes are legion, but I cannot tell them for that would be called interference and that would never do in a Member's Club where every man has a say and every man is a green keeper.

I have been asked many times now that I have given up running a Golf Club, as to what thoughts I have to improve the running of this Club in particular. Firstly one has to think about the person in overall charge of a Golf Club. Who is it? Is it the Chairman? The President? The current Captain? The Secretary perhaps or maybe it is a majority vote for the Club Committee? One must not forget the head green keeper, he at least must have, or should have, first-rate knowledge of actually working the course side of the Club. But supposing for some reason or other your head green keeper is not really up to scratch, then who tells him what he should be doing? Turning that last sentence around a bit, who does the head green keeper ask when he knows he wants a certain article of machinery? For instance his trailer gangs are worn out and he would like the Club to invest in a mounted seven mower arrangement that is controlled by the PTO (power take off). Who would know the hydraulic lifting power of such a machine, let alone any practical knowledge of its pros and cons?

In my case it was easy, it sounds pompous to a degree but I did know the lot and in my opinion the overall power in a Golf Club whether it be a Member's Club or any other type of Club, should be vested in the Secretary, *but* he has to have a working knowledge of *everything* that goes on in his domain. He should liaise with the Chairman of the Club on all important matters but he should not be dictated to by some worthy

Committee man whether he be a peer or a plumber.

There are courses for Golf Club Secretaries and some of them were sent to me for practical training after they had learnt such mundane jobs as cleaning out a beer pipe in the bar and seeing *all* the optics were dead level; the resulting fine by the weights and measure people leaves a lot to be desired. This man or for that matter woman should be seen at times on a tractor or mower or doing something on the course, it need not be hard labour, but the Members appreciate that it is happening and they get the feeling that the person concerned really knows what he is doing.

The ground staff which, if they are backed up with the right tools, should number three and they *must* play golf. Matches *must* be arranged with other green keepers from other clubs and the Home Club should pay for any costs relating to these matches. It is surprising what efforts are then put into *your* course before the match; your men want to show the other what *they* can do.

On the knotty problem of the bar and the catering I think I tried every variation and finally came down to charging every Member a sum on his yearly sub. That sum was handed to the Member concerned on vouchers which could only be spent over the bar or for food. You then had the pleasant job of going round every pub and hotel within a five-mile radius and checking on *their* prices, you then set *your* bar prices at 5% lower and advertise the fact. In the end we got so popular that I had to engage more bar staff, pretty ones, they tend to assist in more ways than one. Prizes were also given in vouchers.

Allocation of duties lay with the Secretary; it was he who 'did' the till in the morning at about 07.00; it was he who did the one-armed gentleman; it was he who took the early green fee ticket and it was he who saw that the staff got in at the prescribed time, although towards the end I installed a signing-in machine which lessened the load somewhat.

I play golf with a couple of working farmers. One, Martin is about forty, and the other, Henry, is in the fifty plus region.

Their continual questions to me, generally when I am about to take a crucial putt is *if* they wanted to make money owning a Golf Club, how would they set about it? Both these chaps are milking about sixty cows and both have in the region of 300 acres, so after missing my putt and losing the round, we retire to the 19th and I ask them for the umpteenth time are they really serious and do they really want to know? If so I want a pint, for it could be thirsty work.

Firstly you are both lucky in more ways than one, in that you own the land necessary to build a Golf Course and even just as important, you are working farmers and eighty hours per week is the norm of your life. For if you want to make money owning and running your own Golf Course, then costs such as salaries can be cut to the bare bone, for most of the work is more or less grassland farming, which you both have been doing all your working life and the same applied to me. The next thing to think about is whether your two farms will actually be able to produce playable courses; for instance, it is not much use if you have houses dotted about your future course; they get in the way in more ways than one.

Then how interesting can you make this future course of yours? If you have small copses, a stream or two or even better a smallish lake, then half the future battle is won. All you have to do now is to decide *where* your future Club House is going to be situated and don't forget that the Club House, Pro's shop and various sheds are all important to the making of a friendly comfortable Golf Course. Having decided where this Club House is going to be, and in that decision you have to consider that you want your first tee within comfortable walking distance of the car park and also just as important you want the tenth tee not all that far away from the first so that the two combine to a certain extent. Next, and this is vital, is the length of the course. Ideally it would be nice to have six par threes, six fours, and six fives which makes a course of par seventy-two, which for the working/profit-making course is too long. Your future customer/Member wants to get round the course in about three to three and a half hours flat and then have time for a reflective pint in the 19th before returning to the golfing widow or the workbench.

I have not the time now, and my pint is dwindling fast, to explain how you work out each hole. You both play golf so that you know the fundamentals of the layout, so that I would leave it to you, *but* it is the workforce which needs explaining. The course you play on, Henry, has at least six full-time green staff, which unless you win the lottery is a waste of money. It takes about two hours and forty-five minutes to mow eighteen greens *and* their counterparts, the winter greens. Likewise, always providing that you have the right equipment, it takes about three hours to mow *all* the fairways and shape them where necessary. So that leaves the semi-rough and of course the rough. The semi-rough which wants to be just slightly longer that the fairways and is generally the width of a mounted set of gangs; i.e. twelve foot, takes all of an hour. The rough, to start with anyway, is generally better tackled with an old silage cutter and a trailer running alongside to cart the unwanted length of grass. You want the rough to be long enough to make playing a shot out of it difficult but *not* impossible, and the rough must *not* be so long that you cannot find your ball quickly. So, for starters, till you get the rough trimmed down to the proper length, that will take three to four hours, bearing in mind that you only have to cut the rough say once a week and the fairways twice, maybe three times a week, one working farmer can get through that lot in quite a casual sort of way.

I have left out the tees which need cutting at least twice a week because this is where your OAP, and I mean just that, comes in. I, when I started and for the first three years did all the above *and* had spare time, but my OAP, one Albert, was also essential. For Albert did the bunkers and caned the greens every morning. Although I could have mown the tees with my mounted mowers with ease, I found it better to buy Albert a motorised bunker rake and also a small three-cylinder mower, so that when he came to a tee, he could shift the pegs a foot *every* day, and mow the thing as well.

Then you come to the vexed question of *greens*, their size, their costs, etc. You can of course go out and buy very costly grass seed and wait at least a couple of years before they are playable, *or* you can, as I did find a firm who grows first-class turf (and mine used to patch Wimbledon), prepare your site and lay down the turf and although you will have tramlines all over the place, it, the green, is fit to be used carefully within *six* months. The fairways, now you are both grassland farmers and you have acres of the stuff, mow it and mow it till the course grasses, cocksfoot and the like, die and the grass becomes finer and finer and there you have your course at a fraction of what the non-farmer pays.

The course where I now belong is thinking of building another nine holes at £16,000 per *hole*. I constructed eighteen holes plus a few practice ones for £6,000. I now deserve another pint. Any further questions?

If you have a completely flat expanse of grass, ideally it would be nice to have a couple of hundred acres with a stream or two in it, plus one or two smallish hills — the cost of that, anything from £500 to £1,500 per acre. Then unless you are capable of doing it yourself, you have to find yourself a Golf Course architect. Frankly I wouldn't like to put a price on that for I never employed one, but it's considerable and then you have the building of the course; eighteen holes, plus probably another nine which could be used as a practice ground for Members who have never played the game (they have to be taught before they are let onto the main course). The cost of the eighteen holes depends a lot on the length of the course. If you want a Championship course of a seventy-two par or more with greens par excellence from the start, *and* you are going to sow costly grass over all the fairways and possibly the rough as well, the mind boggles; the overall cost and the length of time that it would take for the course to become playable, at a very rough guess, some £3,000 to £6,000 per hole.

But if you are a farmer and thus own land and you get this crazy notion that you might just make more money running a

Golf Course than fiddling about with the tits of countless cows, then that is quite a different story. If you are a grassland farmer, then all you want is a decent set of gang mowers, a second-hand JCB and don't sell your silage cutter for a while for you will need it for a few months.

One assumes that you play golf and that your handicap is in the region of 20. Find yourself three friends who are prepared to hit a number of balls from a designated spot; their handicaps should be about 4, 8, 12. Go to the nearest Pro's shop and buy yourself eighty odd balls and then make your first big decision as to where the first tee should go, bearing in mind that the tenth tee and the 18th tee should not be far away. Colour your eighty balls with different colours and then having decided the par (distance) of the first hole *and* the direction, you get your three friends to fire away with their twenty balls. It soon becomes plain as to where the first fairway bunker should be by the various colours of the balls, always assuming that you are wise from the start and that you want to build your course to suit the medium golfer who has a handicap of between 18 and say 24. Do not get led astray and build yourself a course that is so difficult that only the scratch to 12 handicapper has a hope of getting round in four hours plus.

The everyday run-of-the-mill golfer wants to get round the course in three and a half hours flat, which gives him time to have a beer or three in the Club House before going home to the golfing widow. So plan your course for about a par of sixty-eight with an ideal of six par threes, nine par fours, and three par fives; almost impossible to achieve but it's interesting if you can get near that figure, bearing in mind that some, not all, of the par threes should be difficult.

To your greens and their making I used turf, and before the experts hold up their hands in horror, just have a think. Where is the best laid grass in England? I would have a guess at Wimbledon, they at times have to patch their courts. I got my grass or turf from the same place. All the turves were around about twelve years' sown and were superb. The other nice thing about using turves is that, providing you know what you are doing, you can play on them within a period of six little months, whereas *if* you sow grass the seed itself is very costly and it might take two years or more before it can be used as a green.

Then to the making of the tees. Unless you are making some enormous high tee for some reason or other, then make all your thirty-six or more tees the length of a cricket pitch and only about a foot high so that the mounted gangs can, when you are mowing fairways, go over them; it saves hours of work.

Then your 200 acres more or less of grassland. Use your old silage cutters to bring your rough down to about three to four inches, no more; your semi-rough down to about an inch and a half and your fairways down to about an inch. Continue cutting them in that fashion at least twice a week in the growing season and you will find that your old tough farmland grasses, such as cocksfoot and the like, will gradually become fine and in the end you will be able to place your hand flat down on your fairways and the imprint will stay there for a fleeting moment of time.

Have I satisfied your questions about costs? No, there is one last one and that is from a Scot who wants to know what my costs were. I built eighteen holes for £6,000. I acquired a Club House for £4,000 and the automatic water system was in the region of £12,000. On top of that you have some machinery, mowers for greens came to about £3,000, gang mowers about £2,500 and miscellaneous items another £5,000. So for some £30,000 one was in the business but don't forget I am talking about 1967.

Now you ask about profits. For the first three years I broke even, but only just, and there were times when I wondered what I had let my family into. But from the fourth year onwards, when new Members were flocking in, the voucher system after a somewhat sticky start gave me some £12,000 profit on the bar and likewise on the catering; the one-armed gentleman, once the £200 jackpot was introduced, helped considerably. Green fees were in the region of £40,000 and of course one had the normal entrance fees and annual subs. But then one started to differ from the normal (or nearly normal Members' Golf Club), for there was a constant flow of Members who wanted to come sailing and learn navigation and/or deep-sea fishing, and of course they paid for the time concerned. There were Members who wanted to learn fly-fishing; they paid for it. There were Members who wanted to use the gym on the estate; they paid. There were numerous numbers of owners of large lawns near us who wanted their lawns cut by our greens mowers; they paid quite a lot.

Then there was the 'golfing ladder' which was more than popular with the Members. This worked like an ordinary 'squash ladder', the name below you on the ladder played you for the large sum of one pound, but 50p went to me and I paid out quite a large sum, shall we say in excess of £1,000 to the name on top of the 'heap' on Christmas Day.

So now may I please go out with a mate of mine and with the aid of 'Sunningdale' endeavour to extract a quid off him?